A to Z
OF MARRIAGE

KINGSLEY & MILDRED OKONKWO

ISBN 9798386160401

FOREWORD

A-Z of marriage is a matter-of-fact and very precise manual, alphabetically arranged for convenience, to help men and women better understand their needs for a better marriage.

- Kingsley Okonkwo

APPRECIATION

Thank you Diche Enunwa and Bose Samuel-Udeme for making this book a reality. You are proof that with the right partnership one can make anything work

A

ACCEPTANCE

Every man wants to be accepted by his wife for who he is and not for who she hopes he could be. Try to avoid nagging and complaining about everything your husband does. Let him be free to be who he is in your presence. Hard as it may seem, you must learn to accept his aws. Then, you can begin to encourage him to change one step at a time.

ATTENTION

Phone calls, text messages and using her picture as your display picture on any of your social media platforms will tell any woman "I love you." Every woman craves attention. She wants to be noticed.

She wants you to switch off that TV and speak to her. She wants you to pay close attention to her when you ask her what's wrong and not take the first "nothing" she tells you as an actual response. She wants to know that she matters to you.

BEAUTY

Men are moved by what they see. Always make an effort to look beautiful for your husband. Take out time to get your hair done, take care of your skin, lose the pregnancy weight, trim your eyebrows and learn to apply basic make-up to enhance your God-given beauty. Dress nice too. Not every woman is a natural fashionista but you can learn basic colour combinations and what looks good on your body type

B

BRAVE

A story was told of a man who was attacked by robbers in his house. They ordered him to surrender his money or his life. Afraid, he thought he heard the robbers say, "Your money or your wife." So he pushed his wife forward crying "Take her. Take her!" I'm sure you don't want to be that guy. No woman wants to marry a coward. Every woman wants a man that can protect her. So be brave in the face of danger, in the place of prayer and when handling difficult situations. Protect her from your mother if the need arises and please, don't cry when she goes into labour.

CHALLENGE HIM TO BE BETTER

A man wants a woman who can challenge him to be a better man. So nd non-threatening ways to inspire your husband to be a better version of himself. If for any reason you think he is living below his potential, go to God in prayers and ask for wisdom to gently guide him in the right direction.

C

COMPLIMENT HER

"Sweetheart, is it just me or are you getting more beautiful?" This is one of the most wonderful things you can say to your wife. Sometimes, it's just you but nothing scores you more points than a timely compliment to your wife like "What would I ever do without you?" or "Your hair looks amazing." A woman never gets tired of compliments. In case you are thinking "But I told her the food was delicious yesterday. Do I have to tell her again today? Well, you were happy yesterday.

Do you want to be happy again today?

DEVOTED

Be devoted to your husband. Be committed to making his life better at all times. Stick by him through thick and thin. Let him feel like he is the most important person in your life. When you are dedicated to him, no matter the distractions life throws at you, like your job or the kids, you will nd a way to give him your full attention. In a nutshell, learn to make him your "everything" at every time.

Do you want to be happy again today?

D

DESIRE

A man who longs for something he really wants to have like the latest game console, a smart phone or a brand new car, understands the concept of desire. When you want something desperately, you will go to any length to get it. Women need to be wanted and they want you to show it. Your wife wants you to desire her even though you've been married for many years. Hold her, kiss her and initiate sex. Don't always wait for her to reach out to you; always leave your wife without a doubt that you are still attracted to her.

E

ENCOURAGMENT

A man needs massive doses of encouragement. Do not be deceived by his macho demeanour. As his wife, you must be his number one fan and most enthusiastic cheerleader. Encourage him through the rough times; let him know you are with him every step of the way cheering him on till he pulls through.

E

EMPATHY

Being a woman is hard enough. We are faced with monthly periods, pregnancy, nursing babies, cranky tantrum-throwing toddlers, strong-willed teenagers and eventually, menopause. All of these while juggling a marriage, a job, family life and a whole lot of issues. Sometimes, we just want a man who notices all we do and offers some empathy. We need him to help ease the burden, ask how we feel, rub our tired feet and generally show some support.

FRIENDSHIP

A man wants his wife to be his friend. He wants to be able to hang out with you and just relax. He wants to watch a football match or play a video game without having to be constantly reminded of bills and responsibilities. He also wants to let his guard down and confide in you without being scrutinized or criticized.

FOREPLAY

Most men as the Americans say are very "Wham! Bam! Thank you, Ma'am". Once a man gets xated on having sex that is all that really matters to him. Women, on the other hand, are quite the opposite. For us, sex begins long before the actual act. Men are like gas burners while women are like slow burners; they may take a while to heat up. But once they do, it's usually worth it. Take time to touch her, tease her, kiss her slowly and make her feel special.

G

GRATEFUL

Men like it when women are grateful. Men are not as skilled in relational matters as women are. When your husband goes out of his way to do something nice for you, show him how grateful you are for his thoughts and kind gesture. It will go a long way to encourage him and boost his con dence. Appreciate his efforts to make you happy or be a better husband, no matter how little. Trust me, he will de nitely be motivated to do more.

G

GENEROUS

No woman wants a stingy man. You must be generous with your money, your time, your body, just name it. Nothing within your power should be too much to give to your wife. Women are never tired of shopping (wink wink) so spoil her as often as you can afford to, she deserves it.

HELP

This is the main reason you were created (See Genesis 2:18). God didn't just make any kind of help for Adam; He made a help that was suitable and adaptable to him. Find out the exact area(s) your husband needs your help and ll the gap. Be it domestic help, nancial help etc. Whatever the case is, identify and embrace why God put you in his life and get to work. And most importantly, do it with a smile, not grudgingly and with complaints.

HUMOUR

Life is hard enough, especially if you live in this part of the world. Every woman wants a man that can help her laugh through it all as laughter makes marriage more memorable. A merry heart does good like medicine. (Proverbs 17:22). As a husband, you may not be a comedian or even be that funny but you must have the ability to make your wife laugh. Be the kind of man that keeps her laughing and joyful.

I

INTELLIGENCE

Beauty may help you attract a man but intelligence will help you keep the man. A man likes a woman that can stimulate him mentally and be able to have an intelligent conversation. He needs to know that you can hold your own end when the conversation switches from cooking and fashion to politics, sports or business. So read books, listen to the news and keep learning (See Proverbs 11:22 MSG)

INTIMACY

Most women are living with strangers. Yes, you eat the same food, sleep in the same bed and live in the same house with your wife but you are strangers to each other. She wants you to spend time with her; she wants to be your best friend and share your greatest fears and deepest secrets. She wants to be close to you and feel emotionally connected to you.

J

JOVIAL

Men like to have fun. Although they are no longer boys, they still want to play. They like women that are fun and can have fun. As his wife, your job is not to stop him from having fun rather, it is your job is to have fun with him. So don't try to stop him from playing his computer games or even physical games, instead learn how to play them so you can play them with him

J

JUST

Every woman wants a man she can trust to be just, fair and objective in his judgement of tough situations. Sometimes, you will nd yourself in dif cult positions where for instance, your mother and your wife do not get along or your sister and your wife have a misunderstanding. These scenarios always come up and women want to be sure that you will be fair-minded and conscientious.

K

KEMPT

Most men like clean women. Even when a man is not so clean himself, he will still appreciate a clean woman. So take a bath at least twice a day (non-negotiable). Use deodorant, wear clean clothes and underwear and keep the home neat and tidy as well.

K

KIND GESTURES

Everyone could do a little kindness. Sometimes, it's not even the big things. It's the little thoughtful things that scream I love you the loudest. Go out of your way to do things for her. You both go out to work and have a long day. Don't always come home and sit in front of the TV waiting for her to get home and make dinner. Sometimes, surprise her and make dinner, iron her outfit, wash her car, fill her tank and help her with heavy loads. Even learning to use the word "please" would mean a lot. Do something kind for your wife.

L

LOYALTY

Your husband needs to know he has your support at all times. He needs to know that you'll always have his back even when he's going through hard times. It is important that you stand by him through the good and bad times, not just as a bystander, actively ghting for and with him through it all.

LEADERSHIP

Having a great leader as a husband is one of the greatest gifts any woman can have. A leader provides, protects and presides. A good leader will nurture his wife till she is the very best she can possibly be; he will bring out the leader in her. When I met my husband, I had a lot of gifts and abilities that were in me but until he began to push, nurture, guide and show me that I can be better, I would never have achieved half the things I have achieved today. His leadership gave me con dence to do more and be more.

M

MEEK

Meekness means that you are eager to learn and willing to change. A man wants his wife to be teachable, adaptable and open to change. Never be too proud to ask your husband for help when you don't know what to do.

MONEY

Love is good but money makes love so much better. I know you've heard it many times before but let me say it again: THERE'S NO ROMANCE WITHOUT FINANCE. It's much easier to maintain love when the house rent isn't due and children's school fees are paid. Money makes romantic gestures possible. When I rst got married, I knew my husband loved me but he couldn't do as many romantic things as he wanted. Now he can take me on vacations, buy me things I really want and generally spoil me. Why? Money!

Love without money can be frustrating.

NOURISH

Men like good food. It's as simple as that. The stomach has always been and still is one of the roads to a man's heart. Being able to cook is a major plus. But if you can't cook then learn or find a way to make sure there is always good food available for your husband. By the way, noodles and cereals are not considered food by men. We can manage them as appetizers while we wait for the real food to get ready.

N

NONSEXUAL TOUCH

I speak on behalf of all the women of the world when I say these next few words: "DON'T TOUCH ME ONLY WHEN YOU WANT TO HAVE SEX." If you can get this, you would have saved yourself a great deal of stress in your marriage. Women like to be touched; give her a hug, put your hand on her shoulder, hold her hands. And if you are really gunning for gold (wink, wink) give her a massage and let her sleep ... Don't expect to be rewarded with sex that night. Trust me, you will score major points.

O

OVATION

Celebrate your husband. Praise and appreciate all his efforts and don't belittle any of his victories. Don't try to clip his ego instead fan it. Let him feel on top of the world with you. Like Mike Murdock said, "There is a king and a fool in every man, it is the one you speak to that responds to you." Don't only complain when he does things wrong, praise him when he does things right.

O

OPEN AND HONEST COMMUNICATION

Too many times, men tend to sieve the information they give their wives. They usually keep the challenges to themselves but share the victories. Your wife is not your baby sister. She is your partner.

Trust me, she can handle it. Discuss every stage and detail of your life with her. If there's a problem, let her know so she can pray about it. Always be open with her, let her know things exactly as they are.

PRAY

Find out what his dreams are at every stage of his life and always pray about it. The fact that you are one of the people that care about him the most makes every prayer you pray for him a heartfelt one and this makes tremendous power available. (See James 5:16). Remember, faith works by love.

PARTICIPATION

Women want you to be a part of the process. We want you to be involved in the things that concern us like raising the children.

Don't be an absentee husband or father. Sometimes, go for parent-teacher meetings or pick up the kids from school once in a while. Help get them ready for church on a Sunday morning or if you have a baby, offer to do daddy duty once in a while and let your wife sleep. Be a part of raising the children; a part of disciplining them.

We just want you to be involved. Money will never replace your being a part of this at all.

Q

QUIET

Every man likes to have some "me" time. He doesn't want you constantly nagging him. Sometimes, he wants peace and quiet to think and plan. So try not to always be in his face. Give him his space when he needs it. Have a meek and quiet spirit. (See Proverbs 21:9, Proverbs 21:19, Proverbs 25:24)

QUALITY TIME

If your idea of spending time with your wife is sitting in front of the TV watching a football match while she sits beside you talking and you intermittently nod while in all sincerity you didn't hear a word she said then listen up: you are not spending quality time together. Shut down everything. Pay close attention to her. Do what she enjoys doing. Maybe even plan a date night once a week; send the kids to grandma and be with your wife.

RESPECT

One of a man's biggest need is respect. Every man has an in-built ego that requires that you constantly respect him, serve him, talk to him with honour and treat him like your king. A woman must respect her husband on his own terms. If he does not feel respected, then it does not matter how hard you think you are trying, you are not there yet. Never raise your voice when speaking to him, even when you are angry.

R

ROMANCE

Once you get a brand new car, a Toyota, Mercedes or even a Ferrari, if you don't put some fuel in it, it is bound to stop moving at some point. Romance is like the fuel in a marriage. It is not in the expensive or big things you do but in the simple things you do in a special way. It can be a text in the middle of her busy day or stopping by her office to take her to lunch. It can be a weekend getaway after a long week or even a little gift. It's more in the detail and the thoughtfulness.

SEX

I'm sure you guessed this already. Every man needs SEX. A man's sexual appetite is usually far more than a woman can comprehend. He can never have too much sex. So make it available in abundance anytime and every time to your husband. As I always say, if a man has eaten a heavy meal at home, he will not need to buy junk food outside. Selah!

S

SECURITY

One of the major needs every woman has is security. A woman needs her husband to make her feel safe. She needs to know that she can go to bed at night with the assurance that there's someone she trusts who is looking out for her. She wants to be secure spiritually, emotionally and physically. She wants a priest, a faithful lover and a soldier all rolled up in one. A man who will stand in the gap for her, stand faithful to her and stand for her in times of trouble.

TRUST

A man needs to be able to trust his wife. After all, he is going to be eating her food. He needs to be able to give you his passwords and pin numbers without having sleepless nights or tell you a secret without hearing it from a family member or neighbour. (See Proverbs 31:11-12)

T

TRANSPARENCY

Secrets are the cankerworms eating into the fabric of marriages today. Every couple that hides secrets from each other will eventually destroy their marriage. A woman needs a man who will be transparent with her about passwords, pin numbers, past relationships she may need to worry about. Let her know about your work and the businesses you are involved in. Too many wives are left clueless and stranded once their husbands pass on leaving the innocent children to suffer for no reason.

UNITY

Unity is key in marriage. Two are better than one because they have a good reward for their labour. (Ecclesiastes 4:9 KJV) Unity brings results faster than anything else. Once you are in agreement with your husband, good things will start to happen. Remember, if two shall agree concerning anything it shall be done. (See Matthew 18:19) Be involved and committed to his dreams, work with him and support him. Be in agreement with him. (See Amos 3:3)

U

UNDERSTANDING

Men want an understanding wife yet too many of them fail to see that women also want to be understood. For instance, when she says she's tired, she needs you to understand that she might have had a long day and needs you to be patient with her. Don't be a saint to others and a mean terrorist to your wife. Don't crucify her for every single mistake she makes while making excuses for others. Be understanding.

V

VIRTUOS

A virtuous woman is a crown to her husband. She is the kind of woman that once she enters a man's life, he becomes better and he enters into his kingship. Even the Bible emphasizes on the need for a woman to be virtuous; almost a whole chapter is dedicated to her. She is industrious and beautiful but more importantly she is a woman that fears the Lord. A man needs a woman who is strong in all mental and moral capabilities, yet hardworking and well-put together.

V

VISIONARY

A woman wants a man with visions and dreams. Every man should be the prophet of his home; someone who can see the direction in which the family should go. For you to lead successfully, you must be a man with a vision. A woman needs to trust that you know where you are going, that is the only way she can follow willingly.

WISE WOMAN

The Bible tells us that a wise woman builds her home but a foolish one tears it down with her own hands (Proverbs 14:1 NLT). A man wants a woman that can exhibit sound judgement, give him good advice and wise counsel. Someone who can manage certain circumstances without making things worse. He wants a woman that can handle sensitive issues in the family when they arise.

WORKING MAN

A woman wants a man with visions and dreams. Every man should be the prophet of his home; someone who can see the direction in which the family should go. For you to lead successfully, you must be a man with a vision. A woman needs to trust that you know where you are going, that is the only way she can follow willingly.

X

X-FACTOR

The X-factor is that peculiar quality or particular essence that makes you "the one". It is the reason your husband picked you amidst all the other girls. He wants a woman that retains that aura.

X-FACTOR

Some men just stand out. Sometimes, you can't even tell what it is but they just stand out to you. It is that thing she saw in you that made her decide to leave father and mother and forsake all others just to say "I do" to you. Now that she's in your home, don't lose that sense of mystery. She wants to still be in awe of you even if you are her husband.

YIELD

Be submissive; learn to yield to your husband's vision for the family even when you don't agree with him. There is only one captain in the marriage ship. You may gently give your opinions but if he doesn't go with them then pray and support him through his plans.

YERN

Imagine walking in through the door after a long day at work and your wife runs up to you and grabs you into a warm embrace and a kiss that promises many joys to come. You know how you feel?

Exactly! That's the same way a woman wants to feel when she gets home to her husband. She wants to feel like you miss her and love having her around. She wants to know that she's a part of you and not just a piece of furniture.

ZEST

Don't be lazy! Be energetic and active. Every man wants his wife to be hardworking and industrious. Even as a housewife, don't just sit around watching TV all day. Be up and doing in the home. Do something that keeps you busy. No man wants a liability. A purposeful woman is always more attractive to a man.

ZEAL

A man who is passionate about you is like an aphrodisiac. There's no greater feeling for a woman than a man who is always excited to see her and can't keep his hands off her. He's so consumed with his love for her that he's always thinking of ways to love her, excite her and prove his love for her. He leaves her with no doubts that she will always be his number one and that she comes rst to him.

Women want a man that will put them rst because he can't imagine losing her or a life without her.

SURRRERNDER TO CHRIST

If you have not given your heart to Christ, this is a good opportunity to do so. God reserves only good and perfect gifts for His children. Come into God's fold today. Let Him help you become the kind of spouse that you should be. Let him help you ful l your destiny. It's really simple. Just say this prayer from your heart:

Lord Jesus, come into my heart. Forgive me my sin. Wash me with your blood. I receive the grace to serve you all the days of my life.

Thank you Father, for I am born again in Jesus might name, Amen.

Congratulations! Welcome to the family of God.

OTHER BOOKS BY KINGSLEY & MILDRED OKONKWO

- Who Should I Marry?
- When Am I Ready?
- 25 Wrong Reasons People Enter Relationships
- Just Us Girls
- Should Ladies Propose?
- I Love you But My Parents say No
- God Told Me to Marry You
- Waiting For Isaac
- 7 Qualities Wise Men Want.
- 7 Questions Wise Women Ask.
- Chayil - The Virtuous Woman
- Chayil Journal - Praying for your husband

- Help! My Husband is Acting Funny
- Hannah's Heart Devotional
- Simply Attractive.(e-book)
- 21 Days Sexual Purity Devotional (e-book)
- All Year Round for Men
- All Year Round for Women
- Manual: The Way Men Think
- 21 Days Prayers and Fasting For Expectant Mothers. (e-book)

Made in the USA
Middletown, DE
17 March 2025